Erich Wolfgang
KORNGOLD
1897 HIS LIFE AND WORKS 1957
by Brendan G. Carroll

Edited by Konrad Hopkins and Ronald van Roekel

Cover Design and Frontispiece by Craig Maclachlan

ERICH WOLFGANG KORNGOLD
1897-1957
His Life and Works

by

Brendan G. Carroll

't Kan verkeeren.
('Things can change.')

—G.A. Bredero

A RonKon Paperback
WILFION BOOKS, PUBLISHERS
Paisley, Scotland
1984

ISBN 0 905075 15 3

Printed by PDC Copyprint,
         65 High Street,
         Paisley, Renfrewshire,
         Scotland, U.K.

First published in Great Britain by
         Wilfion Books, Publishers
         4 Townhead Terrace,
         Paisley, Renfrewshire PA1 2AX
         Scotland, U.K.

To estimate the greatness of a genius one should not only consider the mistakes or weaknesses of his work and then rate him low; but rather, one should merely take into account the most splendid elements.

—Schopenhauer

CONTENTS

FOREWORD

When I commenced research into the life and music of Erich Wolfgang Korngold, I could not have foreseen that I would become involved in more than ten years of study and international travel. At that time, too, the idea of a major biography of Korngold, to say nothing of a Society dedicated to the preservation and promotion of his music, seemed an improbable dream.

The circumstances in which I came to be associated with Korngold were unusual. When I was a boy, one of my favourite films was *The Sea Hawk*, which was seldom out of the TV schedules, and it was a favourite of mine chiefly because of its splendid music.

One afternoon in July 1972, I saw a whole album of music under the title *The Sea Hawk* displayed in a record shop window. I rushed in to buy it, and discovered that the music was by Korngold, a name I had never heard before.

In an effort to learn something about the man and his compositions, I went to my local library, but could find nothing at all in the music dictionaries and reference works.

Next I wrote to the London office of the record company, RCA, asking for information about Korngold recordings they had released or were planning to release. For six months, I received no answer. Then a letter arrived from New York – from Korngold's son, George, to whom my letter had been forwarded by the London office. The following Autumn, when George Korngold was in London, I went there to visit him. From our first meeting, we were friends, and our friendship has grown steadily ever since. Later, I had the pleasure of meeting Korngold's other son, Ernst, who has also become a cherished friend.

Although George was, at first, a little sceptical when I told him that I would write his father's biography, he has always assisted me in every way. I made several trips to California, staying at the Korngold home, interviewing the composer's surviving friends and colleagues, and examining his manuscripts. In 1980, I assisted the Korngold family in preparing the collection of Korngold's manuscripts for donation to the Library of Congress, Washington, D.C.

During the years of research, I have interviewed over 300 people, written about 2,000 letters, and amassed in my personal Korngold archive countless reviews, articles, letters, books, photographs, tapes and records, as well as almost all of his scores, in the continuing process of piecing together a hitherto only partially documented chapter of modern music history. It is the story of an extraordinary composer who, because of the caprices of political history and musical fashion, became the victim of unjust neglect.

In October 1982, The Erich Wolfgang Korngold Society was founded in Paisley, Scotland. Here, at last, was an opportunity to bring together in organised membership Korngold's admirers the world over. The Society is administered from the office of Wilfion Books, Publishers, the publishers of this monograph and of my forthcoming full-length biography of Korngold.

This monograph offers the reader a sketch of Korngold's life, and commentaries on seven of his major works, besides a catalogue of his concert, chamber and operatic works, and lists of his operetta arrangements and film scores. The 'Epilogue' chronicles Korngold-related events since the composer's death in 1957, including the most important dates in the Korngold Revival from 1972 to 1985, as far as the facts are known at this writing. Finally, a Selected Discography and a Selected Bibliography are given to direct the reader's attention to some of the recordings of Korngold's music and some of the research sources on Korngold that are presently available.

The aim of this monograph is, therefore, to serve as a mini-reference work on Korngold for his admirers, and perhaps to win him new friends as well — the number of his friends has been growing, as has his reputation since his music was rediscovered about twelve years ago.

And it is not only the music of Korngold that has been rediscovered, but also that of such composers as Franz Schreker, Alexander von Zemlinsky, Max von Schillings, Franz Schmidt, Hans Pfitzner, and Egon Kornauth, to name only a few. If our interest focuses on Korngold, it is not to minimise the achievements of these other men, but in the hope that the study of him will encourage other researchers to investigate their lives and works as well as the entire musical era in which they flourished, that has for too long been either underrated or ignored.

— Brendan G. Carroll
President
THE ERICH WOLFGANG KORNGOLD SOCIETY

Liverpool, England
March 1984

ERICH WOLFGANG KORNGOLD
His Life
29 May 1897–29 November 1957

At the turn of the century, the post-Wagnerian style culminated in the music of Richard Strauss and his contemporaries. The second generation of the Late Romantic German School was largely disregarded by post-World War II musical scholarship, and only in recent years has the legacy of music by such composers as Franz Schreker, Alexander von Zemlinsky, Franz Schmidt, and Erich Wolfgang Korngold been given some degree of the recognition it deserves.

Korngold was born in Brünn (now Brno, in Czechoslovakia), in the province of Moravia, in the Austro-Hungarian Empire, on 29 May 1897, the son of Dr. Julius Korngold, who became the successor to Eduard Hanslick as chief music critic of the Vienna journal, the *Neue Freie Presse*. His vitriolic pen, his hostility to the New Viennese School, and his frequent altercations with Richard Strauss and other leading musical figures provided the substance of a good deal of the coffeehouse gossip in pre-World War I Vienna.[1]

Young Korngold was a composing *Wunderkind*, endowed from an early age with amazing creative gifts. Mozart, Schubert and Mendelssohn are the most famous examples of composing prodigies and their achievements are well documented. The unique aspect in the case of Korngold is the complexity and sophistication of his musical idiom.

He composed in a densely chromatic style, which is the logical extension of the post-Wagnerian school, beyond Richard Strauss and Franz Schreker, but not into the territory explored by the serialists. His musical language is idiosyncratic and receives its impetus from his frenetic rhythms. The combination of these elements, deployed on a large orchestra with brilliant technique, and coupled with an exceptional melodic gift, identifies his artistic uniqueness, which was fully formed in him from the age of ten, when he composed his cantata *Gold*.

As Ernest Newman wrote in *The Nation* in 1914:

> Mozart and Korngold are two geniuses who began to write music in their earliest childhood. Why does Mozart spontaneously lisp music in the simple idiom of his own day, while Korngold lisps in the complex idiom of his? Korngold can hardly have derived his harmonic system from the study of other composers, for in what composer's work could he have found it? It is the spontaneous product of a most subtly organised brain which at the first span embraces practically all we know and feel today in the way of harmonic relation.

Worried about the effects of having a musically precocious son, Dr. Korngold took the boy to Gustav Mahler, who had just resigned as director of the Vienna Opera. A close friend of the Korngolds, he was regarded by Dr. Korngold as the greatest living composer.

After hearing the young Korngold play his cantata *Gold* from memory, Mahler declared that he was 'a genius', and recommended that he be taught by Alexander von Zemlinsky, a composer whom Mahler greatly esteemed. The boy had received some elementary instruction from Mahler's old teacher, Robert Fuchs. His lessons with Zemlinsky, however, precipitated an acceleration of his musical development – 'by the month', as Zemlinsky wrote to Dr. Korngold – and before the year was over, Korngold was orchestrating Beethoven sonata movements with, as Robert Fuchs observed, 'an ease that would have put to shame a student of twenty'.

Composed when he was eleven, Korngold's Piano Sonata No.1 in D minor was as audacious harmonically as Alban Berg's sonata composed (but not published) in the same year (1908-09); and his next work, a two-act ballet-pantomime entitled *Der Schneemann* ('The Snowman'), was given at the Hofoper, in Vienna, in the presence of the Emperor Franz Josef, in October 1910. It became an unqualified success all over Europe, being performed on over thirty stages.

Artur Schnabel introduced his Piano Sonata No.2 in E major, completed when Korngold was thirteen. The Austrian pianist immediately included it in his repertoire, performing it in many European cities. Composed in the grand manner, it was described by the late Canadian pianist Glenn Gould as being 'the blue-print for what might well have made one of the better symphonic essays of its time'. The writing is indeed orchestral, indicating the talent inherent in the young Korngold, who would soon develop into one of the most accomplished orchestrators of his day.

His Piano Trio, Op.1, also completed at the age of thirteen, was performed by Bruno Walter, Friedrich Buxbaum, and Arnold Rosé. Its maturity prompted Felix Weingartner to write to Dr. Korngold, 'It seems as if nature has amassed all her gifts into the cradle of this extraordinary child; may God preserve his health.'

Zemlinsky left Vienna for Prague, and young Korngold went to study counterpoint with Hermann Grädener in 1911. Zemlinsky sent Korngold a postcard, which read: 'Dear Erich, I hear you are studying with Grädener; is he making any progress?'

His first orchestral piece was the *Schauspiel-Ouvertüre*, written when he was fourteen. It was first performed by Arthur Nikisch with the Gewandhaus Orchestra in Leipzig, an unprecedented honour for an adolescent boy. The *Ouvertüre* and his four-movement Sinfonietta (composed when he was fifteen for an orchestra not much smaller than the one used for *Elektra*) caused Richard Strauss to adopt him as a protégé, with these words in a letter to Dr. Korngold: 'Such mastery fills me with awe and fear. May he develop his powers to the full in a normal way.'

Strauss and other musicians who performed and championed his works were confronting a composer of the greatest maturity and finesse, who was still a child. He was called 'the new Mozart', and his powers of musical expression were not confined to composition. He was a remarkable pianist, able to draw orchestral sonorities from the instrument in a most original manner. Besides possessing absolute pitch, he had a superb musical memory. According to his father in his unpublished memoirs, he was able to 'retain in his memory whole scores played on the piano and would freely copy them as if from a picture, fixed in his head'. Years later, in California, Arnold Schoenberg, who was discussing his own Op.23 piano pieces with Korngold, was surprised when Korngold went to the piano and played them from memory, displaying an intimate knowledge of the music which he had not seen for thirty years.[2]

The growing analogy between Korngold and Mozart became embarrassing to Dr. Korngold, who had many enemies. From the beginning, it was rumoured that the father had written the music for the son, an allegation dismissed by Dr. Korngold with the rebuttal, 'If I could write such music, I would not be a critic.'

Korngold consolidated his success with three major works which he composed in his middle-teens, just before the outbreak of the First World War.

The first was a one-act 'opera-buffa', *Der Ring des Polykrates*, based on a short text by Heinrich Teweles, which was a delightful example of Korngold's talent for the theatre. Concise and melodic, it contains the memorable aria, 'Kann's heut nicht fassen', sung by the principal soprano.

But *Polykrates* was too short to be performed alone, and rather than risk pairing it with an incompatible opera by another composer, Korngold, in 1914, began work on a one-act tragedy entitled *Violanta*, to a libretto by the Viennese playwright Hans Müller (1882-1950), brother of Ernst Lothar (two of whose poems Korngold set to music and included among the four songs of his *Abschiedslieder*, Op.14) and a close friend of Dr. Korngold. Müller had previously supplied the texts for Korngold's *Märchenbilder*, Op.3, seven fairy-tale pictures for piano, composed in 1910.

The story of *Violanta* concerns a grande-dame of 15th century Venice who vows to avenge the suicide of her sister, whom the handsome Alfonso, Prince of Naples, had abandoned. During the Carnival, she finds Alfonso and lures him to her room, where her husband, Simone, is to kill him when she sings the blasphemous Carnival song; but she, too, falls in love with Alfonso, and when her husband appears, dagger drawn, she throws herself between the two men and dies of the knife wound that Simone inflicts upon her.

For *Violanta* Korngold composed a score of great sensual power, with high tessitura passages of immense difficulty, brilliant double choruses, and a densely chromatic harmonic structure. Throughout the opera's seventy minutes' duration, the music is in a state of constant ferment, with, as the musicologist Richard Specht noted, 'the scent of repressed passion, a dichotomy of love and hate'.

Korngold was a born dramatist. His father recalled, in his unpublished memoirs, how in *Violanta*

> Erich...with an unfailing dramatic instinct, improved motivation,
> increased intensity and rearranged scenes to tighten the plot. It was
> Erich who insisted on a 'breather', a quiet episode, after the passionate

duet between Violanta and her husband, in which...Violanta, in front of a mirror, is dressed by her old nurse, Barbara.... This break increases the tension, creates the stillness before the storm and propels the action towards the tragic climax.

He began to compose the work in 1914 and finished it at the family country retreat in the Salzkammergut, in the summer of 1915. While holidaying in Alt-Aussee, Korngold played excerpts from the opera score, on a piano, to hotel guests. Among them was Baron Clemens von Franckenstein, director of the Munich Opera, who immediately arranged for the premières of both *Violanta* and *Der Ring des Polykrates* in Munich under Bruno Walter, who later recalled in his autobiography, *Theme and Variations* (1946):

> The experience of hearing the young Korngold play and sing for me the two operas which I was going to perform, I shall never forget. One might have compared his interpretation of his own works on the piano to the eruption of a musico-dramatic volcano, were it not that the lyrical episodes and graceful moments also found their insinuating expression in his playing.

The Munich premières occurred on 28 March 1916; and on 10 April 1916, the two operas received their Vienna premières. The lead soprano for *Polykrates* was Selma Kurz, the foremost coloratura of the time. The sensation of the evening, however, was Maria Jeritza, who sang Violanta. One of the great beauties of her era, she brought the same powerful sexuality to the rôle which made her performances of Salome, Carmen, and later, Turandot, so outstanding. A sceptical Viennese public was completely conquered. She repeated her success in 1919, when *Violanta* was staged for the fiftieth anniversary of the Vienna Imperial Opera, and she also sang the rôle in New York in 1927.

Once again, Korngold was the most discussed composer of the day. Heinrich Kralik, the Viennese critic, wrote in the *feuilleton* the day after the premières: 'Two one-act operas of genius — astonishing examples of a precocious operatic talent, equally capable of seriousness and gaiety.' Richard Strauss spoke of 'the incredible many-sidedness of Korngold's genius', and Egon Wellesz wrote of *Violanta* in *Neuen Tag* (30 March 1916) that 'the powerful sensuality fascinates with its magical orchestral sounds'.

One of Korngold's special gifts is his ability to grip the attention of his audience in the opening bars of a work. In *Violanta*, he does so with an almost Tristanesque chord, embodying an augmented triad (a feature of his music) — the 'Violanta' chord, mysterious, questioning, foreboding.

Violanta is built around melodic and chordal motifs rather than themes. Only Alfonso's aria, the Carnival song, and the final love duet are essentially orthodox. In all his operas, Korngold occasionally gives the voice a division of bars separate from that of the accompaniment, a practice initiated by Richard Strauss. Developing as it progresses, the music regenerates with constantly shifting perspectives on each motif, such as the one depicting Violanta's hate, a spasm of ascending minor triads which intermittently shiver across the orchestral canvas during much of the first half of the work. This 'hate' motif concludes the opera, spiralling to a crashing G minor chord.

Another feature of the music is its idiosyncratic harmonic language. The dense chromaticism of Strauss and Mahler is extended and enlarged.

Korngold's style, especially his harmonic system and melodic writing, is strong and personal, while his orchestration, although undeniably of the Late Romantic School, is instantly recognisable by the use of harps and keyboard instruments, the spacing of the woodwinds, and the string writing. Like many great composers, he reused the same thematic material in different works; one finds themes from early works in music from his latter years. A passage from *Violanta*, coming immediately after the climactic duet in Scene 4, is echoed in his Symphony in F sharp major of 1949-50; and the main theme of the Symphony had already appeared in another form in his opera *Das Wunder der Heliane*, composed 1923-27.

The vast orchestra in *Violanta* is so deployed as to supply, in effect, a symphonic poem surging in the background, commenting on the action and maintaining an elastic yet relentless rhythmic drive. The use of bells and other sonorous effects, including the piano, adds to the overall sensuality of the orchestral sound.

The child prodigy had matured into a front-rank composer who was a serious rival to Richard Strauss as an exponent of German *verismo* opera. Strauss himself, in his 'testament' which he left as a model for the German repertoire, acknowledged Korngold's achievement by naming *Der Ring des Polykrates* in his list of recommended operas.

The third work which contributed to Korngold's reputation as a serious composer was the String Sextet, Op.10, which was premièred under the direction of Arnold Rosé on 2 May 1917. In the years up to the Second World War, it was frequently performed, usually coupled with Schoenberg's *Verklärte Nacht*, as it was again during the Korngold concerts held in Berlin in September 1983.

When the First World War broke out, Dr. Korngold was eager to protect his son from the conflict, but the youth was eventually drafted into the Austrian army in 1917. The doctor who conducted his medical examination had been a voice specialist to many of the singers of the Hofoper, and having spotted Korngold waiting, asked him, 'Do you already have your B classification?', meaning exemption from service at the front. Korngold answered, 'No,' and the doctor said, 'We'll see to it.' He did so, and to the relief of Dr. Korngold and most of Vienna, the young soldier was made musical director of his regiment.

Since the job kept him at home, he was able to continue his creative work. It is almost certain that he began work on his next opera *Die tote Stadt* in 1916, and in 1918, he composed the incidental music to *Much Ado about Nothing* for a performance of the Shakespeare play at the Schlosstheater in Schönbrunn Castle. The production was so successful that it was transferred, on 24 May

1920, to the Vienna Burgtheater, where it continued its successful run. When the orchestra had to keep another engagement elsewhere, Korngold quickly arranged the music for piano and violin (to be played by himself and Rudolf Kolisch), so that the run would not be interrupted. Later, this arrangement was incorporated into the repertoires of Kreisler, Elman, Seidl, and Heifetz, among other violinists, and it was much recorded.

On 4 December 1920, his opera *Die tote Stadt* ('The Dead City') was premièred simultaneously in Hamburg, under Egon Pollak, and in Cologne, under Otto Klemperer.

This three-act expressionistic opera, with a plot embracing supernatural elements and dream-like hallucinations, is the most famous and enduring of all Korngold's works for the musical stage. The libretto (based on the novel *Bruges-la-Morte* by the French-language Belgian author Georges Rodenbach) was attributed to a certain 'Paul Schott', but the name was fictitious. The true identity of 'Paul Schott' was Erich Korngold himself in collaboration with his father, and the pseudonym is a combination of 'Paul', the name of the principal male character in the opera, and the publisher of the opera, B. Schott's Söhne in Mainz, to whose senior partner, Dr. Ludwig Strecker, the work is dedicated. To avoid speculation about the authorship of the opera itself, the identity of 'Paul Schott' remained a closely guarded family secret until *Die tote Stadt* was revived in New York in 1975.

After the double première, the opera opened in Vienna in January 1921, with Maria Jeritza creating the demanding dual-rôle of Marie/Marietta. The principal aria, 'Gluck, das mir verblieb', also known as 'Marietta's Lute Song', became one of the most frequently recorded arias of 20th century opera. Jeritza chose *Die tote Stadt* for her American début at the Metropolitan Opera in New York in November 1921. The opera played in over eighty houses, under the guidance of such conductors as Hans Knappertsbusch, Georg Szell, Artur Bodansky, and Robert Heger. The recording of it under Erich Leinsdorf has reaffirmed its success in our own time, as has the recent production of it by the Deutsche Oper Berlin.

During the 1920s, the incessant controversies surrounding Dr. Korngold were a continual source of embarrassment to the young composer, and his position as guest conductor at the Vienna Opera under the new regime of Franz Schalk and Richard Strauss was made increasingly difficult.

In addition, Arnold Schoenberg and his disciples, who advocated the twelve-tone system, created further difficulties for Korngold, whose music, despite its chromatic nature, was essentially tonal and melodic. Anton Webern wrote bitterly to Schoenberg about the number of performances of Korngold's music while his own was seldom played.[3]

Only Alban Berg evinced admiration for Korngold, and would have liked to form a proper artistic relationship with him, but Dr. Korngold ended the association.[4] And significantly Korngold's set of piano caricatures satirising Stravinsky, Schoenberg, Bartók, and Hindemith was never published.

Korngold's troubles with his father also affected his private life. He had fallen in love with Luzi von Sonnenthal (the grand-daughter of Adolf von Sonnenthal, the great Viennese actor) and proposed to marry her. Paternal opposition was strong, on the grounds that this beautiful and cultured young woman was not good enough for Korngold. He realised, however, that no woman would be considered 'good enough', and regardless of the objections, the couple was married in 1924. The union was a happy one, lasting until Korngold's death in 1957.

Another source of friction between father and son was Dr. Korngold's attempts to influence his son's compositions if he felt they were becoming too 'modern', and to discourage his appreciation of modern music, as when he restrained the young man from applauding *Petrouchka* at its Vienna première. There was also a period of six months when Korngold and his father did not speak to each other.

One of Dr. Korngold's criticisms which did seem valid was directed at his son's decision to accept commissions to arrange operetta scores. These began with Johann Strauss the Younger's *Eine Nacht in Venedig* (for Hubert Marischka) in 1923, and later included two works by Leo Fall and Offenbach's *Die schöne Helena (La Belle Hélène)*, as well as other operettas by Johann Strauss. Korngold accepted these commissions because, once he had married, he had a wife and then a young family to support.

Eine Nacht in Venedig had never been a success until Korngold transformed it by adding other Strauss numbers and tightening the plot structure, and the subsequent adaptations he did were successful, too, but Dr. Korngold believed that his son was wasting his time on such chores. The truth is, however, that apart from earning money, Korngold enjoyed arranging and conducting this light music, regarding the effort involved as a pleasurable diversion from his own composing.

In the 1920s, Korngold's original compositions were few but important. The concert overture *Sursum Corda* ('Lift Up Your Hearts') also received its première in January 1920. It was his only work to be criticised for being 'too modern'. In the form of a one-movement tone poem, it is a heroic work, which Korngold dedicated to Richard Strauss.

In 1922, he began to compose his Quintet for Piano and Strings, Op.15, as well as his String Quartet No.1, Op.16. In 1923, the one-armed pianist Paul Wittgenstein commissioned him to compose a concerto for piano (left-hand) and orchestra. A one-movement work of both stark dissonance and lyrical beauty, it was premièred at the Vienna Music and Theatre Festival on 22 September 1924, with Wittgenstein as soloist and Korngold conducting. Pleased with the concerto, Wittgenstein commissioned a second work from Korngold, who wrote for him a five movement suite for piano (left-hand) quartet.

Also in 1924, the Rosé Quartet performed the String Quartet No.1 in Vienna, and later, the Kolisch Quartet gave it at the International Festival of New Music in Venice, where, according to David Ewen in *The Jewish Tribune*,[5] it caused a furore.

And in Berlin, Korngold recorded his four *Abschiedslieder* ('Songs of Farewell') with Rosette Anday (they had been premièred by Maria Olczewska in November

1921), which are perhaps his finest songs, deserving of a permanent place in the repertory of the German *lied*. Richard Neutra regarded them the equal of Mahler's songs,[6] and they form a direct link with a tradition going back to Schubert.

In 1923, Korngold acquired the manuscript of *Die Heilige*, a mysterium by Hans Kaltneker (1895-1919). Kaltneker's poetry fascinated Korngold, who felt an affinity with the tragically short-lived poet. He transformed the text into the opera *Das Wunder der Heliane*, to a libretto by Hans Müller. Years later, Korngold learned from Dr. Margaret Stegler, a close friend of Kaltneker, that the poet had intended the work to become an opera by Korngold.

Heliane is, in many ways, the most extraordinary work in the Korngold canon. It is scored for immense forces and the harmonic language is complex and uncompromising, much more ambiguous than in *Violanta*, verging on bi-tonality in its constantly shifting modulations that restlessly rob the ear of key centres yet retain a firm tonal base.

The opera was premièred in Hamburg on 7 October 1927 under Egon Pollak, and on 29 October in Vienna under Franz Schalk. It was not a success, however. The public, hoping for another *Die tote Stadt*, were not prepared for an opera on the theme of the mystical celebration of eternal love. Moreover, backstage intrigues and a quarrel between Dr. Korngold and the supporters of Ernst Křenek's opera *Jonny spielt auf* that raged in the Press for weeks prior to the première increased public antipathy to *Heliane* and its composer, who, nonetheless, always considered it to be his masterpiece.

After completing *Heliane*, Korngold began teaching Opera and Composition at the Vienna Staatsakademie, and was awarded the title of 'Professor Honoris Causa' by the President of Austria. A poll conducted by the *Neues Wiener Tagblatt*, in 1932, named Korngold and Schoenberg as the two greatest living composers.

In 1929, he began an artistic collaboration with the Austrian theatrical producer-director, Max Reinhardt, for his new production of *Die Fledermaus* in Berlin. Korngold interpolated other Strauss music to enrich the score, but to mollify the purists, he played these pieces himself on the piano at every performance, a gesture which always delighted the audiences.

He had known Reinhardt since the days of *Der Schneemann*. In 1926, Reinhardt asked him to write incidental music for his production of Schiller's *Turandot*, but he refused the offer because of the impending première of Puccini's opera of the same title. When Reinhardt was invited by Warner Bros. to make a film version in Hollywood of his stage production of Shakespeare's *A Midsummer Night's Dream*, he took Korngold with him to supervise the music. The rising tide of Nazism in Europe (Hitler was elected Chancellor of Germany in January 1933) was an added incentive to Korngold, who was Jewish, to go to Hollywood, accompanied by his wife, in 1934. For the next few years, he divided his time between Vienna and Hollywood, but when the Germans occupied Austria in 1938, Korngold stayed on in America, not returning to Europe until 1949.

Music in the cinema had been one of the last developments when sound films arrived in the mid-twenties. The marrying of two soundtracks, music and speech, was a considerable technical problem to solve, but by 1933 brief musical interludes and 'title music' were beginning to be accepted. In Hollywood, in the same year, Vienna-born Max Steiner (1888-1971) more or less revolutionised the industry's ideas on music in films when he composed the mood music for *King Kong*.

In 1931, Korngold had been approached by Erich Pommer at UFA, the leading German film studio, to write the score for the film *Der Kongress tanzt*, but he declined (it was eventually composed by Werner Heymann). When Reinhardt presented Korngold with another opportunity to work on a film, however, he readily accepted it.

Reinhardt wanted to use Mendelssohn's *A Midsummer Night's Dream* music in its entirety, but Korngold realised that there was not enough of it to underscore the whole film, nor did it, in Korngold's estimation, provide sufficient variety for the different segments of the film. Korngold's solution was to interpolate several other pieces by Mendelssohn, particularly from *The Songs without Words*, one of which he arranged for Titania to sing as a lullaby to Bottom. In addition, he composed linking passages in the Mendelssohn style to unify the score.

His innate mathematical ability enabled him to calculate the exact amount of music required per foot of film. When he was being shown around the studio for the first time by Henry Blanke (the assistant producer on the Reinhardt film), Korngold asked how long one foot of film would last on the screen. Upon being told by a technician, he remarked, 'Ah, exactly as long as the first two measures of the Mendelssohn Scherzo.' His sense of timing was renowned throughout the industry. He composed precisely the correct amount of music to a finished film, and while recording the music, he never used a stop-watch, cue-sheet, or any other timing device.

The music for *A Midsummer Night's Dream* was applied in three layers: 1) by being recorded to the finished film as it was shown on the screen; 2) by being performed on the set so that the actors would be aware of how to play a scene; and 3) by having Korngold on the set 'conducting' the actors in the rhythmic utterance of the dialogue to match the music.[7] This process was unprecedented in 1935, and it earned Korngold the respect and admiration of musicians and film specialists alike.

Furthermore, his gift for swift delineation of dramatic subjects, first demonstrated in his ballet-pantomime *Der Schneemann*, and later developed in his operas, was now applied to film-music writing. This gift involved creating individual leitmotifs for each main character in the film, and a musical undercurrent to provide atmosphere and dramatic nuance to accompany the action on the screen. The 'operas without singing', as Korngold called his film scores, are all marked by a nobility of design and a brilliantly structured content, and they often enhanced the films beyond the producers' expectations.

Between 1933 and 1937, Korngold also composed his new opera, *Die Kathrin*. The protracted schedule was due in part to the commissions he received to write film scores. By late 1937, he had established himself as the leading composer of symphonic film music in America. His first original film score was for *Captain Blood* in 1935, and his score for *Anthony Adverse*, in 1936, won an Academy Award. Two further film projects with Reinhardt, *Danton*[8] and *The Miracle*, were abandoned, but he was offered the chance to score *The Adventures of Robin Hood*. He hesitated, then returned to America from Vienna in January 1938, having learned that neither Richard Tauber nor Bruno Walter would be available until the Autumn for the Vienna première of *Die Kathrin* (which, suppressed by Hitler, received its belated world première in Stockholm on 7 October 1939). On 12 February 1938, he accepted the assignment to score *Robin Hood*, the same day that Austrian Chancellor Schuschnigg met Hitler, an event that opened the way for the *Anschluss* on 13 March 1938.

The fall of Austria deeply depressed Korngold. It also meant that those members of his family still in Vienna were in extreme danger. After several anxious days, however, he was notified that they had escaped across the border into Switzerland. Two weeks later, his property was confiscated by the Nazis ('for his numerous debts' was the official explanation), and although Dr. Korngold had managed to rescue some of his son's precious manuscripts, the bulk of the music library, including all of Korngold's childhood sketches and original autographs, were left in the house in the Sternwärtestrasse at the mercy of the invading troops.

Korngold cabled Weinbergers, the music publishers (with whom he was dealing at the time), who had an office in Vienna, and to their eternal credit, they sent two employees to the house after midnight to retrieve the manuscripts, which had been dumped in the cellar to await incineration, while German soldiers caroused upstairs. Disassembled and hidden between the pages of printed music to be exported to the United States, virtually the entire collection of manuscripts was saved for posterity. In the summer of 1980, the present author inventoried the collection in Los Angeles before it was donated by the Korngold family to the Library of Congress in Washington, D.C., in December 1981.

As soon as the manuscripts crisis was resolved, Korngold began composing the score for *The Adventures of Robin Hood*, and completed it in seven weeks. It won him his second Academy Award, and remains to this day one of the most successful examples of blending music and visuals.

During the war years, Korngold supported his family as well as refugees from Europe with his earnings from composing film scores and working with Reinhardt on his stage productions, which included the American versions of his operetta arrangements.

Among the films he scored, *The Constant Nymph* (1943) deserves special mention. For it he composed a symphonic tone poem for contralto, chorus and orchestra entitled *Tomorrow*, which was later published as his Opus 33. In response to the many requests for the music, that Warner Bros. received, it was recorded by the Warner Orchestra with Clemence Groves for Decca in 1944, but owing to war-time shellac shortages, the recording was never released.

Korngold's own favourite among his scores was *Between Two Worlds* (1944), a film based on Sutton Vane's play *Outward Bound*. Its mystical, semi-religious plot about a group of people in transit between life and death, and awaiting final judgements, appealed to Korngold. The score is reminiscent of *Das Wunder der Heliane*, especially in the closing scenes where an ecstatic theme expressing the bond of love between the characters played by Paul Henried and Eleanor Parker is almost a variation on the aria 'Ich Ging zu Ihm' from *Heliane*.

For *Deception* (1946), Korngold composed a one-movement cello concerto, which he later expanded and published as his Opus 37. It was his last original film score.

His farewell to film work occurred in 1954, when Korngold agreed to supervise and arrange Wagner's music for the film-biography of Wagner called *Magic Fire*, made in Munich, with William Dieterle directing. Although the script was poor, the musical contributions at least were distinguished. When Wagner and Liszt played a piano duet together, Korngold recorded both tracks, and he made his first and only appearance in a feature film as the conductor Hans Richter, seen briefly on the podium in one scene.[9]

Listening to his film scores, one is never conscious that the music is merely filling in or marking time. It is dynamic music, continuously developing and evolving, with complex thematic interplay. At times the music sweeps the film along, pacing the drama, identifying the characters, accentuating the moods, and heightening the atmosphere. Perhaps the truest test of the value and durability of his scores is that in the recent recordings of them, where the music is divorced from the screen images, they still sound fresh, powerful, convincing, and inspiring.

In 1945, Dr. Julius Korngold died after a long illness. His death marked the close of an epoch for Korngold. To his father's dismay, he had vowed not to compose any more absolute music until, in his words, 'that monster in Europe is removed from the world', and so his father did not live to witness his son's return to the concert world.

For Christmas 1944, however, Korngold presented his wife with a special gift – sketches for his String Quartet No.3 (the String Quartet No.2 had been written in 1935). With this chamber work began his late period, when he was to write some of his finest compositions.

Early in 1945, Bronislaw Huberman urged him to write a violin concerto, but Huberman died before he could perform the work (Op.35), which Jascha Heifetz later played successfully in public and in a recording. Encouraged by this success, Korngold resumed his concert career. The Cello Concerto, the Serenade for Strings, and a song cycle followed in 1946-47; and in 1949, he returned to Vienna, hoping to take up his professional life where he had left it eleven years earlier.

But post-war Europe did not welcome the returning composer. The artistic environment was at odds with Korngold's philosophy, and the new musical trends were incompatible with his melodic, tonal style. On his way through Europe, Korngold learned of the death of his former mentor, Richard Strauss, who had invited him for a reunion. This event, more than any other, symbolised the demise of everything that Korngold and his generation had represented before the war.

With the rapid rise of the serialists to musical dominance, the neo-Romantics had become unfashionable. Mahler and his contemporaries were condemned as passé and long-winded, and Korngold was additionally stigmatised for being a film composer. He was regarded not as a serious composer of integrity, but merely as 'a Hollywood slush artist', an insulting label that still attaches to him today.

Returning to Vienna, which was no longer the centre of the arts that it had once been, Korngold found the musical climate completely changed and most of the critics hostile towards him. The faithful few who remained had neither the authority nor the influence to stimulate a Korngold renaissance.

Even though the Vienna première of his Serenade for Strings, Op.39, under Furtwängler, in 1950, was a success, from then on until his death the critics were merciless in their disparaging reviews. When the Vienna Opera announced a revival of *Die tote Stadt*, Korngold's hopes were raised, only to be dashed after an intrigue involving the double casting of the rôle of Paul without the knowledge of either tenor, led to the cancellation of the production. *Die Kathrin*, too, had to overcome several obstacles and postponements before it was finally premièred in Vienna in October 1950. Dismissed by the critics as 'old fashioned', it nevertheless was greeted with forty curtain calls on its opening night. But negative reviews and dwindling audiences resulted in the opera being taken off. Relentlessly the critics attacked his music – even his Violin Concerto, which had had an enthusiastic reception in America and Europe,[10] was ridiculed because 'composition has travelled a long way from the idea of just writing some warm romantic tunes', as one critic put it. Performances were infrequent, and few professional musicians would endorse his works. Many of his followers were now dead, or had emigrated, and a whole generation had grown up without knowing that he existed.

Even so, always the optimist, undaunted and undeterred, Korngold set about resuscitating his career. In 1949, he had started work on a Symphony in the unusual key of F sharp major. Works in this key are rare – Messiaen's *Turangalîla* and Mahler's unfinished Tenth Symphony are two other examples – but for Korngold it was a favourite key.

The Symphony was his last major work and his supreme orchestral creation, a synthesis of his musical personality. The language is streamlined, precise, and pointillistic, alternately harsh and heroic. His style had undergone continuous development from its earliest expression; the original percussive, rhythmic element now blossomed fully in this logical symphonic extension and expansion of his idiom.

Explaining his musical philosophy, Korngold wrote in a letter to Dr. Herman Lewandowsky in 1952:

> I believe that my newly completed symphony will show the world that atonality and ugly dissonance and the price of giving up inspiration, form, expression, melody, and beauty will result in ultimate disaster for the art of music.

This philosophy is inherent in all of Korngold's music, and while the Symphony is a 20th century work, it remains true to Korngold's distinctive melodic style, which many contemporary musicians consider anachronistic.

The Symphony was to be ignored for over twenty years. Among the Korngold papers inventoried in Los Angeles were found letters of rejection from the many conductors to whom Korngold had offered his Symphony for a first performance.

Unable to muster any support and weakened by a heart attack, Korngold continued to compose anyway. He produced sketches for a second symphony and planned a sixth opera to be based on a dramatisation by Gerhart Hauptmann of a story, *Das Kloster bei Sendomir*, by Franz Grillparzer, but he did not live long enough to complete either work.

Erich Wolfgang Korngold died of a cerebral haemorrhage, in Los Angeles, on 29 November 1957, aged sixty. In his honour, the Vienna Opera House flew the black flag of mourning at half-mast. On being told of this gesture, his widow stared blankly into space for a few moments and then murmured, 'It's a little late.'[11]

For fifteen years after his death, Korngold's reputation was in eclipse. In 1959, Dimitri Mitroupolis wrote of the Symphony in F sharp major: 'All my life I have searched for the perfect modern work. In this symphony I have found it. I shall perform it next season.' His death intervened, however, and the work was not performed in concert until 1972, when Rudolf Kempe conducted it in Munich, although it had been performed on European radio several times.

That same year, RCA records released an album of his classic film scores that met with astonishing success and led to a renewed interest in his concert and operatic music. Suddenly, the flood gates opened to a Korngold Revival which has been gathering momentum ever since.

In 1974, the first recording of the Symphony, under Kempe, appeared; in 1975, *Die tote Stadt* was revived in New York, and was recorded under Erich Leinsdorf's direction; the 1980 recording of *Violanta*, conducted by Marek Janowski, was an international success; and in 1981, Christopher Keene conducted the St. Louis Symphony Orchestra in a performance of the Symphony in F sharp.

The U.K. première of the Symphony took place in March 1982 with the Royal Liverpool Philharmonic Orchestra under Marek Janowski. To commemorate the occasion, the Scottish sculptor Alexander J. Stoddart was commissioned to create a portrait-bust of Korngold, which was exhibited at the Philharmonic Hall, Liverpool, on the day of the première, and is now on permanent display in the Deutsche Oper Berlin.

The Erich Wolfgang Korngold Society was founded in October 1982 to promote interest in Korngold's music and serve as a focal point for the composer's admirers throughout the world.

Then, in February 1983, the Deutsche Oper Berlin mounted a new production of *Die tote Stadt*, produced by Professor Götz Friedrich, and starring Karan Armstrong as Marie/Marietta and James King as Paul. A month later, in New York, the one-act opera *Der Ring des Polykrates* was revived at the Manhattan School of Music.

Sender Freies Berlin presented a Korngold retrospective in collaboration with the Berlin Radio Symphony Orchestra, Gerd Albrecht, conductor, in September 1983. Among the Korngold works performed were the Piano Trio, the String Sextet, the Sinfonietta (all of which were recorded for release on the Varese Sarabande label in 1984), and the Concerto for Piano (Left-Hand) and Orchestra, with Steven de Groote as soloist.

Varese Sarabande also released an album of the score for *The Adventures of Robin Hood* in December 1983, and in early 1984, the same label issued the original soundtrack of *Magic Fire*, complete with piano excerpts recorded by Korngold and extracts from Wagner's operas sung by Leonie Rysanek and Marianne Schech, among others.

On 8 February 1984, the Violin Concerto was played by Ingo Klöckl in Wiesbaden, and will be given again by Christian Altenburger with the Chicago Symphony Orchestra in November. Further performances of *Die tote Stadt* have been scheduled by the Deutsche Oper Berlin for later in 1984, while in the Summer, *Violanta* will be presented together with Zemlinsky's one-act opera *Eine florentinische Tragödie* by the Santa Fe Opera in New Mexico, U.S.A.

Korngold's film music will receive concert performances, too, when the Detroit Symphony Orchestra performs *The Adventures of Robin Hood* and selections from *Captain Blood*, *Robin Hood*, and *Kings Row*, in two separate programmes in August 1984.

Plans for performances of Korngold's music in 1985 are now being made, including the American première of the Left-Hand Piano Concerto with the New York Philharmonic Orchestra, under the direction of Zubin Mehta, and Gary Graffman as soloist; and of *Sursum Corda* by the Scottish Sinfonia, Edinburgh, under Neil Mantle.

The works of Erich Wolfgang Korngold are once again being heard in live concerts and in opera houses, as well as on recordings. His achievement, for many years obscured, is on the point of complete vindication, and will at last be assured of its rightful place in the history of 20th century music.

1   Paul Bechert, 'The Korngold Scandal', *Musical Times* (London, 1922).

2   Related to the author by Ernst Korngold.

3   Hans Moldenhauer, *Anton Webern* (New York, 1980).

4   Related to the author on 5 March 1976, in Paris, by Dr. Edwin Eisler, former Director of the Royal Opera House, Graz, Austria.

5   Published in the U.S.A., 2 December 1927.

6   Letter from Richard Neutra to his mother, dated 20 March 1920, given to the author by Frau Dione Neutra.

7   See article written by Korngold published in *Music and Dance in California*, June 1940.

8   One theme written for *Danton* was used in the Panama sequence in *The Sea Hawk* (1940).

9   Korngold's only other film appearance, in which he played the piano, was in *A Dream Comes True*, a short promotional film for *A Midsummer Night's Dream*, in 1934.

10 The Violin Concerto was given its European première in Vienna on 30 June 1947, with Bronislaw Gimpel, soloist, and Otto Klemperer, conductor.

11 Luzi Korngold died in 1962.

ERICH WOLFGANG KORNGOLD
His Works
Seven Commentaries

1. Piano Trio in D major, Op.1 (1909)

The Piano Trio, dedicated to his father, was Korngold's first published work.[1] Premièred in Munich on 4 November 1910, by the Schwarz Trio, it received its first performance in Vienna one week later, with Bruno Walter at the piano. Mahler's brother-in-law, the violinist Arnold Rosé, leader of the Vienna Philharmonic, and the cellist Friedrich Buxbaum completed the trio. Arnold Rosé, who led the Rosé Quartet, greatly admired the young composer ever since he had played the violin solos in his ballet-pantomime *Der Schneemann* in October 1910. He performed nearly all of Korngold's chamber music, and Korngold dedicated his String Quartet No. 1 to him, in 1922.

When first performed, the Piano Trio was called modernistic, harmonically audacious, and even *avant-garde* music. Today, however, it seems to be a lyrical work stemming from traditional roots.

The confident opening theme of the First Movement instantly grips the attention. Receiving its impetus from a descending augmented fourth (tritone), it pervades the entire movement and, indeed, the work as a whole. Cyclicism dominated Korngold's formal designs, and in many of his major works, thematic unity and cyclic recapitulation (especially in the finales) play an important part. The piano writing is personalised, echoing the sound of Korngold's own pianistic style, while the harmonic language is equally idiosyncratic, pushing tonality to its furthermost boundaries, yet always returning to a solid tonal base.

The Scherzo recalls the tritone in the short introduction, but the main theme, wayward and rhapsodic, is typical of the Korngold scherzo idiom, and in its dynamic range points ahead to the Piano Sonata No.2 in E major, Op.2 (1910).

The bittersweet Trio, a slow 2/4 in F major, dominated by sevenths, achieves a satirical effect reminiscent of Schoenberg's cabaret style in *Pierrot Lunaire*, although the language is totally different.

The Larghetto in G is an eloquent soliloquy. The cello introduces the theme unaccompanied, culminating in the third phrase in an affecting melody of rising fourths and fifths, a characteristic of many Korngold themes. The theme undergoes several transformations, until it reaches a rapturous cantabile statement to a delicate arpeggio accompaniment by the piano. The coda, combining diminished sevenths suspended over the tonic chord, peacefully concludes the movement.

As the Finale commences, the brusque opening allegro is actually the cello theme of the Larghetto, which leads to a Rondo of two themes. The second theme, in parallel sixths, is marked *Amabile a giocoso*. Then Korngold, displaying his formal mastery, combines all the major themes of the previous movements into a kind of Roundelay, which whirls to a thundering climax crowned with a whole-tone glissando. In the appoggiatura of the final chords all the main themes of the preceding movements are concealed, and the final chord contains the opening tritone from page one of the score, bringing the work to a resounding conclusion.

2. Sinfonietta in B major, Op.5 (1912)

The term 'sinfonietta' is defined in the *Oxford Musical Companion* as 'A symphony on a smaller scale, either in length or in orchestral forces, or both'. The most notable example of the sinfonietta is by Janáček, although excellent works in this *genre* by Alexander von Zemlinsky (who was Korngold's teacher) and Franz Waxman (who was Korngold's colleague at Warner Bros.) also deserve mention.[2]

Korngold's Sinfonietta is neither small-scale nor lightly scored. In this instance, the term refers to the mood and character of the music, typified by the motto theme which appears on the title page and which dominates the four-movement scheme of the work. Entitled *Motiv des Fröhlichen Herzens* ('Motif of the Cheerful Heart'), this theme is an ascending melody built on rising fourths. It takes numerous forms in nearly all of his major compositions, from the score of the ballet-pantomime *Der Schneemann* through the operas, and also in such film scores as *Anthony Adverse*, *The Adventures of Robin Hood*, and *Between Two Worlds*. Scored for a large orchestra, including an expanded percussion section, piano and celeste, this work is truly symphonic, but with a youthful exuberance and gaiety which are both uplifting and endearing – hence, the term Sinfonietta.

The First Movement, in sonata-form structure, begins firmly in the tonic major with a statement of the motto theme. An outstanding feature of this work is its intricate motivic polyphony. Even in the opening statement, development begins in the third phrase, as the fourths are reversed à la retrograde inversion, while the second subject, in G, also conceals the fourths of the principal theme. The development section is replete with fanfares of trumpets and horns, and the climax leads to the recapitulation and the thoughtful coda.

The Scherzo, prefaced by a short introduction enabling a modulation from C to B-flat major, is a musical explosion written brilliantly for timpani and brass, filled with soaring grandeur. Korngold's scherzo idiom relies on jaunty, angular themes, with heavy dynamics and vigorous accentuation. Throughout the Scherzo, the motto theme is always in the background, before it comes forward in the Trio in F sharp major (a favourite Korngold key), where it receives a varied treatment, melodically expressive as it unravels itself modulating through many keys. Korngold weaves from this material a symphonic texture, as the motto theme emerges triumphantly in a rich statement scored for brass, and then fades away. After an abbreviated recapitulation of the Scherzo, the coda ends with hammered strokes alternating between Bs and B-flats.

In the Andante (in G minor), the opening dominant ninth chord sets the sensuous mood of this movement. Divisi strings and the bell-like tones of the celeste support the pensive melody introduced by the cor anglais; the music is mysterious, almost impressionistic, with the motto theme hidden in the pizzicato bass of the strings. As in all of Korngold's slow movements, the emphasis is on sonority, and the harmonic language colours the sparse thematic material. The second theme, for strings, is another variation on the motto theme, this time filled out by a harp accompaniment. The movement closes as, in the final bars, the five notes of 'The Motif of the Cheerful Heart' are sounded by the harp, glockenspiel and woodwinds, harmonised by augmented triads.

The Finale begins in the minor key (*Patetico*) in a strident statement of the motto theme, which proceeds to a fugal treatment of what becomes the principal subject. The fugue dies away; then suddenly, the main idea bursts forth in the tonic major. The song-like second subject, derived from this main theme, is treated operatically, as if it were a love-motif. The development is full of complex interplay, with the motto theme weaving in and out, and even becoming an ostinato bass supporting the main theme on horns, celeste and piano. Dissonance plays its part, too, but in Korngold it is deployed for colouristic effect, not for a specific harmonic purpose. Following the recapitulation, the conclusion is, in the words of the critic Richard Specht, 'a symphonic Song of Songs...'.

3. String Sextet in D major Op.10 (1914-15)

Korngold's finest chamber work, the Sextet is a descendant from the musical world of Brahms and shows a greater affinity with his two essays in this medium than with its immediate antecedent, Schoenberg's *Verklärte Nacht* ('Transfigured Night'), which is in the same key.

Combining the melodic sweetness of Late German Romanticism with the imagery of the Viennese *Jugendstil*, the Sextet is at the same time stamped with Korngold's distinctive personal idiom. The musical language has advanced in complexity from the Piano Trio, but again cyclic interplay controls the formal scheme. The introductory triplet figure (for the second viola), also recalling the interval of the tritone, has the characteristic of a fugal subject. Soon the main theme (for principal violin) sings out, expanding and developing for nearly thirty bars, in a series of unorthodox, intervallic modulations which typify what Puccini described as 'the lovely, unusual unexpected melody'. A climactic recapitulation bridges to a beautiful subsidiary theme in B major. The external development, complete with Fugato section, leads to the sonorous conclusion.

The Adagio comes next. The unaccompanied cello enunciates the main theme, which seems like a development of the Larghetto from the Piano Trio, while the double and triple stopping and the bi-tonal harmony look ahead to the Adagio of the String Quartet No.1. The mood is intense, as the simple thematic material is enriched by constant modulations to distant keys, punctuated by bizarre chord structures that rob the ear of a key centre, yet always return to consonant tonality.

The Intermezzo, a graceful 6/8 in F major, is one of the most appealing pieces that Korngold ever wrote. The principal theme is a variation of the motto theme from the Sinfonietta, a long-spanned, elegiac, yet unpredictable melody. The musicologist and composer Nicolas Slonimsky once wrote of Korngold that 'his music represents the last breath of the romantic spirit of Vienna', and nowhere in Korngold's works is this spirit more audible than in this Intermezzo. The conclusion, where the violin whistles, as it were, the melody one last time, while everything slips away 'like a dream in a moonlit night' (in the words of a contemporary writer), is finished with a Korngoldian cadence that is magical.

The Finale, like all Korngold finales, is high-spirited and good-humoured. Some of the thematic material derives from the preceding movements, while the second subject, jaunty and robust, prefigures the Finale of the Symphony in F sharp major, Op.40, composed over thirty years later. There is homogeneity in Korngold's music, a force of creative continuity. His musical personality is exhibited in a variety of profiles and perspectives in his varied output, yet it remains unmistakeably Korngold.

4. *Abschiedslieder*, Op.14 (1920)

Although Korngold composed songs before and after the *Abschiedslieder*, these four 'Songs of Farewell' are the most significant examples of the *genre* that he produced. In his first three operas, *Der Ring des Polykrates*, *Violanta*, and *Die tote Stadt*, he had developed his talent for writing effective lyric pauses, and these songs are closely related to the major arias from these works.

Based on poems by Dante Gabriel Rossetti (adapted by Alfred Kerr), Edith Ronsperger, and Ernst Lothar, the songs are given a highly orchestral piano accompaniment that is of equal importance with the voice. Typically, the chord and interval of the seventh are prominent, and the vocal line is wide-ranging and demanding. The score is unusually detailed in terms of expression and dynamics; there are only two bars in the cycle where Korngold does not make some instructive remark: he leaves nothing to chance.

The first song, 'Sterbelied' ('Requiem') in B-flat major, has some very difficult intervals (elevenths and twelfths), and portamento is used copiously. Piquant harmonies penetrate the intense atmosphere, punctuating the long-spanned melodic line.

The second song (in C major), 'Die Eine Kann mein Sehnen nimmer fassen' ('This one thing is not understood by my yearning'), is scherzo-like and the most operatic of the set.

The third song (in E major), 'Mond so gehst Du wieder auf' ('The Moon Has Risen'), is sublime and tragic. Its resigned, deeply felt mood is reminiscent of Mahler's *Kindertotenlieder*. Korngold used it again as the basis for a variation movement in his Piano Quintet, Op.15 (1921-22), which also includes quotations from the other songs in this cycle.

The final song, 'Gefasster Abschied' (in E-flat major) ('Serene Farewell'), is another variation of 'The Motif of the Cheerful Heart', and derives from the earlier 'The Austrian Soldier's Song of Farewell', written in 1917. It brings the cycle to an end with a hushed air of calm simplicity.

The songs were completed for Christmas 1920. The first performance was given by Maria Olczewska in November 1921, and in 1923 Rosette Anday gave the first performance of the orchestral version of the cycle, with Korngold conducting. She later recorded them, with the composer at the piano.

5. String Quartet No.1 in A major, Op.16 (1922)

Of Korngold's three string quartets, the first one is the fiercest and most intense. The First Movement, with its rushing, agitated first subject, is rhythmically emancipated. In contrast, the lyrical second subject is serene. It reappears in the last movement, another example of Korngold's cyclicism in development.

Korngold achieves a quasi-orchestral sound in this quartet, as in the Sextet, by a constant use of double and triple stopping, and this is especially so in the Adagio. It opens in bi-tonal ambiguity, before resolving itself in the tonality of C major. The recurring dissonant motif, which haunts this movement, has a parallel in the Adagio of the Symphony in F sharp major.

The Intermezzo contains a certain melodic phrase as its main theme, which reappears in many ways throughout Korngold's works, such as the Third Movement of the Piano Sonata No.3 (1930) and in the Main Title to the film score for *Elizabeth and Essex*. In the String Quartet No.1, it is heavily embroidered with pizzicato semi-quavers.

The Finale, which bears the quotation 'When birds do sing,/ Hey ding a ding ding,/ Sweet lovers love the Spring' (from *As You Like It*), is yet another variation on the motto theme from the Sinfonietta. Here it is a romantic song, giving way to a joyful march for the second subject. The second half of the second subject is distantly related to the 'Hornpipe' from the incidental music to *Much Ado about Nothing*. The conclusion is a terrific climax, with all the instruments pausing on an extended trill, before the final cadence.

The String Quartet No.1 was premièred by the Rosé Quartet, in Vienna, on 6 January 1924, and the following year, it caused controversy at the International Festival of New Music in Venice. The Chilingirian Quartet gave its first performance in the U.K. in December 1976, and afterwards recorded it for the RCA label.

6. *The Adventures of Robin Hood* [3] (1938)

This is perhaps Korngold's most representative film score. In it he utilised the principal motif from his concert overture *Sursum Corda*,[4] Op.13 (1919-20), as the leitmotif for Robin Hood. A heroic theme, it bears some resemblance to 'The Motif of the Cheerful Heart', and is in the same mould as the themes from the tone poems of Richard Strauss (to whom *Sursum Corda* is dedicated).

At some point in its composition, Korngold must have decided to make his score for *Robin Hood* into a symphonic poem, and the similarities between Robin Hood and Don Quixote, Don Juan, and the hero of *Ein Heldenleben* were probably not lost on him. To this end, he incorporated much more of *Sursum Corda* into the film score than he originally planned. For Robin's escape from Nottingham Castle after the Banquet, he used a complete segment of the earlier work, inserting connecting links wherever necessary. Elsewhere, he used a subsidiary theme for one of the love motifs for Robin and Maid Marian. Finally, for the main love theme, which also served as the motif for Richard the Lionheart, he used a variation on the motto theme from the Sinfonietta.

The rest of the score – fast-paced and rhythmically elaborate – is a feast of melody and orchestral display to complement the exciting action on the screen.

After the Main Title, which combines the March of the Merry Men and the Lionheart theme, a brief scene establishing the evil of Prince John and his partner-in-crime, Sir Guy of Gisbourne, moves swiftly to a montage of the ignominies inflicted on the hapless Saxons. One of them, a miller, is arrested for shooting a deer in Sherwood Forest. About to be clubbed, he is saved by Sir Robin of Locksley, and for the first time the *Sursum Corda* motif rings out. The principal trumpet player with the Warner Orchestra, Larry Sullivan, played this difficult theme with a virtuosity and power unmatched in subsequent recordings.

The music propels the film from scene to scene, at the same time identifying each character with his or her own leitmotif. Especially memorable is the music for Friar Tuck, a wistful, mysterious religioso, with decorative flutes and bell-like effects. In the Archery Tournament, the fanfares of rising fourths conjure up a picture of medieval splendour, while the music in the Treasure Wagon sequence reproduces the effect of the outlaws jumping from the trees onto the soldiers.

The supreme glory of the score, however, is the Coronation, Duel and Victory sequence, for which Korngold augmented the normal orchestra with a separate brass choir. The Duel music, in particular, is remarkable, so closely does it follow and emphasise the action on the screen, and even without the film, this fierce scherzo is a thrilling composition.

Indeed, the whole score is impressive music without the screen images. Listening to it in the new recording by the Utah Symphony Orchestra (on the Varese Sarabande label, No.704.180), one does not sense that anything is lacking. Closely knit into a symphonic mesh, the themes are developed throughout the score. Because it is 'through-composed', it would be possible to play each segment in chronological order, as the cues are tightly connected, with key relationships always correctly observed.

7. Symphony in F sharp major, Op.40 (1949-50)

Korngold's only symphony, this work in four movements is scored for a large orchestra, including piano, celeste, marimba, and harp. The chromatic nature of F sharp major suited Korngold's melodic and harmonic style.

The discordant, percussive opening of the First Movement, *Moderato, ma energico*, is one of the most arresting to any symphony. It leads to the principal theme, a long and complex inspiration for B-flat clarinet, which emanates from a rising seventh and extends over nearly fifty bars. The second subject is lyrical. Its march-like development is pointillistically scored and tensely dramatic. Then the subject becomes a fanfare for horns. After a condensed recapitulation, the movement ends in a sombre mood, the opening chords played by the strings *col legno*, crowned with the chord of F sharp played by the full orchestra.

The Scherzo is a tarantella demanding articulate virtuosity; the second subject is a heroic theme for four horns (again built on fourths and fifths). The Trio, in contrast, is sparse, ghostly, and eerily chromatic. It is a simple descending chromatic figure which travels through numerous modulations.

The Adagio in D minor is based on a three-note motif, which is varied and developed for some twenty-eight bars. There are two secondary themes, one a rising scale, the other a descending chromatic figure. Although the mood of the movement is tragic, the three ecstatic climaxes suggest sensuousness as well.

The joyous Finale recalls in cyclic references all the preceding movements. Its principal theme is the lyrical second subject of the First Movement, now transformed into a humorous dance-like tune for flute and piccolo, answered by a warm, syncopated cello melody. Hidden in the orchestral fabric, too, of course, is Korngold's motto theme from the Sinfonietta. The work ends in the brilliant key of F sharp major.

1 His earlier works were published privately and subsequently brought out by Universal Edition.

2 Among the many other composers who have written orchestral works with the name 'sinfonietta' are Benjamin Britten, Francis Poulenc, Albert Roussel, Malcolm Williamson, Eugene Goosens, and Sergei Prokofiev.

3 For the complete script and a discursive article on the film and its production, see *The Adventures of Robin Hood* by Rudy Behlmer, published by the University of Wisconsin Press.

4 *Sursum Corda*, a Latin invocation from the Roman Catholic Mass, means 'Lift Up Your Hearts'.

CATALOGUE OF WORKS BY ERICH WOLFGANG KORNGOLD

1. **1906**   *Gold.* A dramatic cantata for soli, chorus, and piano. (Mss. lost.)

2. **1907-08**   *Don Quixote: Six Characteristic Pieces for Piano*

3. **1908**   Caprice Fantastique for Violin and Piano.

4. **1908**   *Der Schneemann.* Two-act ballet-pantomime. Libretto by Erich Wolfgang Korngold.

5. **1908-09**   Piano Sonata No.1 in D minor

6. **1909-10**   Piano Trio in D major, Op.1

7. **1910**   Piano Sonata No.2 in E major, Op.2

8. **1910**   *Märchenbilder,* Op.3. Seven piano pieces. Text by Hans Müller.

9. **1911**   *Schauspiel-Ouvertüre* in B major, Op.4. For large orchestra.

10. **1912**   Sinfonietta in B major, Op.5. For large orchestra.

11. **1912**   Sonata for Violin and Piano in G major, Op.6

12. **1913-14**   *Der Ring des Polykrates,* Op.7. One-act opera-buffa. After a text by Heinrich Teweles. Libretto (uncredited) by Leo Feld and Julius Korngold. Première: Munich, 28 March 1916.

13. **1914-15**   *Violanta,* Op.8. One-act opera. Libretto by Hans Müller. Première: Munich, 28 March 1916.

14. **1911-13**   *Einfache Lieder,* Op.9. Six songs (poems by Eichendorff, Honold, Kipper, and Trebitsch).

15. **1914-15**   String Sextet in D major, Op.10

16. **1917**   Military March. For large orchestra.

17. **1917**   Hymn for Empress Zita. For chorus and orchestra.

18. **1917**   'Austrian Soldier's Song of Farewell'

19. **1918**   *Much Ado about Nothing*, Op.11. Incidental music to Shakespeare's play.

20. **1919**   'Ode to a Goose-Liver in the Haus Duschnitz'. Text by Erich Wolfgang Korngold. (Mss. only.)

21. **1916-20**   *Die tote Stadt*, Op.12. Three-act opera. Libretto by Paul Schott (Erich Wolfgang Korngold and Dr. Julius Korngold), after the novel *Bruges-la-Morte* by Georges Rodenbach. Premières: Hamburg and Cologne, 4 December 1920.

22. **1919-20**   Symphonic Overture for Large Orchestra: *Sursum Corda*, Op.13

23. **1920**   *Abschiedslieder*, Op.14. Four songs (poems by Rossetti-Kerr, Ronsperger, Lothar).

24. **1921-22**   Piano Quintet in E major, Op.15

25. **1922**   String Quartet No.1 in A major, Op.16

26. **1923**   Concerto for Piano (Left-Hand) and Orchestra in C sharp Op.17. Commissioned by Paul Wittgenstein and premièred by him, 1924.

27. **1924**   *Drei Lieder*, Op.18. Three songs (poems by Hans Kaltneker).

28. **1926**   *Four Little Caricatures for Children*, Op.19. (Mss. only) Piano pieces satirising Stravinsky, Schoenberg, Bartók, and Hindemith.

29. **1923-27**   *Das Wunder der Heliane*, Op.20. Three-act opera. Libretto by Hans Müller, after mysterium *Die Heilige* by Hans Kaltneker. Première: Hamburg, 7 October 1927.

30. **1927**   *Tales of Strauss*, Op.21. For piano.

31. **1927**   *Drei Lieder*, Op.22. Three songs (poems by K. Kobald).

32. **1930**   Suite for Two Violins, Cello, and Piano (Left-Hand), Op.23. Commissioned by Paul Wittgenstein.

33. **1931-32**   *The Baby Serenade*, Op.24. In five movements. For salon orchestra.

34. **1931**   Piano Sonata No.3 in C major, Op.25

35. **1933-35**   String Quartet No.2 in E flat major, Op.26

36. **1934**   *The Eternal*, Op.27. Song cycle (poems by E. van der Straaten).

37. **1933-37**   *Die Kathrin*, Op.28. Three-act folk opera. Libretto by Ernst Decsey. Première: Stockholm, 7 October 1939.

38. **1939**   *Songs of the Clown*, Op.29. For contralto and piano. Settings of songs from Shakespeare's *Twelfth Night*.

39. **1941**   Psalm for Chorus and Orchestra, Op.30. On Hebrew prayers by Jacob Sonderling. (Mss. only.)

40. **1941**   Four Shakespeare Songs, Op.31. Settings of songs from *Othello* and *As You Like It*. (Mss. only.)

41. **1942**   Prayer for Chorus, piano, Organ, and Tenor Solo, Op.32. (Mss. only.)

42. **1942**   *Tomorrow*, Op.33. Symphonic Poem for Orchestra, Contralto, and Chorus. Text by Margaret Kennedy.

43. **1944-45**   String Quartet No.3 in D major, Op.34

44. **1945**   Violin Concerto in D major, Op.35

45. **1946**   *The Silent Serenade*, Op.36. Vocal score, scenic overture and incidental music to two-act stage comedy by Erich Wolfgang Korngold. Libretto by Bert Reisfeld.

46. **1946**   Cello Concerto in C major, Op.37

47. **1946**   Romance Impromptu for Cello and Piano, Op. Posth.

48. **1947**   *Fünf Lieder*, Op.38. Five songs (poems by Dehmel, Eichendorff, Koch, and Shakespeare).

49. **1947**   Symphonic Serenade for Strings in B-flat, Op.39

50. **1949-50**   Symphony in F sharp major, Op.40

51. **1949**   *Sonett für Wien*, Op.41. For contralto, with piano accompaniment. Setting of poem by Hans Kaltneker.

52. **1955**   *Theme and Variations*, Op.42. For orchestra.

Additional Compositions[1] without Opus Numbers:

1. **1913**   *Der Sturm*. For large orchestra and chorus. Tone poem to a text by Heinrich Heine.

2. **c.1914**   Four Little Waltzes, for Piano.

3. **1919**   Dance in Old Style. For small orchestra.

4. **c.1922**   *Der Vampir*. Incidental music to a play by Hans Müller. For chamber orchestra.

5. **c.1948**   Waltz for Luzi in the style of Chopin. For piano. (Composed for his wife.)

6. **1953**   *Straussiana*. In three movements, for orchestra. A potpourri of famous Johann Strauss melodies.

7. **19??**   Miscellaneous *lieder*, piano pieces, chamber pieces, vocal and instrumental fugues, and choral pieces

---

1   Of these compositions, only number 6, *Straussiana*, has been published to date. Also, Dr. Rudolf Stefan Hoffmann, in his monograph *Erich Wolfgang Korngold* (Vienna, 1922), mentions a Piano Scherzo by Mendelssohn which Korngold orchestrated delightfully in 1917 and performed in 1922, but neither the score nor details of the performance have yet come to light.

OPERETTA ARRANGEMENTS BY ERICH WOLFGANG KORNGOLD

Johann Strauss the Younger:

1. 1923   *Eine Nacht in Venedig*

2. 1926   *Cagliostro in Wien*

3. 1929   *Die Fledermaus*

4. 1931   *Walzer aus Wien*

5. 1932   *Das Lied der Liebe*

6. 1942 and
   1947   *Rosalinda* (American version of *Die Fledermaus*)

7. 1949 and
   1953   *The Great Waltz* (American version of *Walzer aus Wien*)

Jacques Offenbach:

1. 1931 and   *Die schöne Helena (La Belle Hélène)*
   1944   *Helen Goes to Troy* (American version of *Die schöne Helena)*

Leo Fall:

1. 1929   *Rosen aus Florida*

2. 1933   *Die Geschiedene Frau* (in Mss. only: lost)

Additional:

1. 1941   Incidental music and songs to *At Your Service*, based on Rossini, for Max Reinhardt's production of *The Servant of Two Masters* by Goldoni (in mss. only).

FILM SCORES BY ERICH WOLFGANG KORNGOLD

The dates refer to the years in which the films were released.

1. **1935**   *A Midsummer Night's Dream*. Arrangements of music by Felix Mendelssohn, with some original linking passages.

2. **1935**   *Captain Blood*

3. **1936**   *Give Us This Night*. Includes miniature opera, *Romeo and Juliet*, sung by Gladys Swarthout and Jan Kiepura.

4. **1936**   *Rose of the Rancho*. One song.

5. **1936**   *Anthony Adverse*. Academy Award.

6. **1936**   *The Green Pastures*. Two orchestral sequences: The Creation and The Flood. Uncredited.

7. **1936**   *Hearts Divided*. One scene only. Uncredited.

8. **1937**   *Another Dawn*

9. **1937**   *The Prince and the Pauper*

10. **1938**   *The Adventures of Robin Hood*. Academy Award.

11. **1939**   *Juarez*

12. **1939**   *The Private Lives of Elizabeth and Essex*

13. **1940**   *The Sea Hawk*

14. **1941**   *The Sea Wolf*

15. **1942**   *Kings Row*

16. **1943**   *The Constant Nymph*

17. **1944**   *Between Two Worlds*

18. **1946**   *Devotion*

19. **1946**   *Deception*

20. **1946**   *Of Human Bondage*. Music composed in 1945.

21. **1947**   *Escape Me Never*. Music composed in 1945.

22. **1954**   *Magic Fire*. Arrangements of music by Richard Wagner.

EPILOGUE: Chronology of Korngold-Related Events, 1957-1985

1957   29 November: death of Erich Wolfgang Korngold in Los Angeles, California

1959   November: Memorial Concert in Hollywood

1961   Commemorative album of Korngold's film music issued by Warner Bros.

1962   29 May: an Erich Wolfgang Korngold Memorial Concert at the Los Angeles Conservatory of Music

Death of Luzi Korngold

1966   **Performance of *Der Ring des Polykrates* on radio in West Germany**

1967   *Der Ring des Polykrates* and *Die tote Stadt* performed at the Volksoper, Vienna

Publication of *Erich Wolfgang Korngold*, memoir by Luzi Korngold, in Vienna

1969   *Die tote Stadt* performed in Ghent, Belgium

1970   Three performances of *Das Wunder der Heliane* in Ghent, Belgium

1972   Symphony in F sharp major, Op.40, performed by Munich Philharmonic Orchestra, Rudolf Kempe conducting, in Munich

The Sea Hawk: The Classic Film Scores of Erich Wolfgang Korngold released by RCA

Brendan G. Carroll commences researching his biography of Korngold

1973   *Elizabeth and Essex: The Classic Film Scores of Erich Wolfgang Korngold* released by RCA

1974   *Classic Film Scores for Bette Davis* released by RCA: contains 'Elizabeth' from *Elizabeth and Essex* and 'Carlotta' from *Juarez*, both by Korngold

Symphony in F sharp major, Op.40, Munich Philharmonic Orchestra, Rudolf Kempe conducting, released by RCA

Violin Concerto in D, Jascha Heifetz, soloist, re-released by RCA

Violin Concerto in D, Ulf Hoelscher, soloist; *Viel Lärm um Nichts* ('Much Ado about Nothing') Suite; and *Thema und Variationen* ('Theme and Variations'), Radio Orchestra Stuttgart, Willy Mattes conducting, released by EMI

1975　　June: *Die tote Stadt* revived in New York

Captain Blood: Classic Film Scores for Errol Flynn released by RCA: contains selections from *The Adventures of Robin Hood*, *Captain Blood*, and *The Sea Hawk*

1976　　*Die tote Stadt*, Erich Leinsdorf conducting, released by RCA

Much Ado about Nothing Suite, Westphalian Symphony Orchestra, Recklinghausen, Siegfried Landau conducting, released by Vox Turnabout

6 December: Brendan G. Carroll directs first Korngold concert in Great Britain in 17 years, an evening of chamber music, at Christ's College, University of Liverpool

1977　　String Quartet No.1 in A major and String Quartet No.3 in D major, Chilingirian String Quartet, released by RCA

1978　　First public performance of *Four Little Caricatures for Children*, Op.19 (1926), given by Michael Young, pianist, in Liverpool, and broadcast by the BBC

1979　　*Die tote Stadt* performed in cut version in Darmstadt, West Germany

1980　　*Violanta*, Marek Janowski conducting, released by CBS Masterworks

Kings Row Suite, Charles Gerhardt conducting, released by Chalfont Digital

The Korngold family decide to donate music mss. collection to the Library of Congress, Washington, D.C.

Brendan G. Carroll inventories the collection in Hollywood

1981 Donation of the mss. collection completed

Kings Row music played at the Inauguration of Ronald Reagan as President of the United States

April: Brendan G. Carroll's talk on Korngold broadcast on 'Music Weekly' programme, BBC Radio 3

CBS Masterworks recording of *Violanta* broadcast on BBC Radio 3

Wilfion Books, Publishers (Paisley, Scotland) decide to publish Brendan G. Carroll's biography of Korngold

Schauspiel Overture, Op.4, M.I.T. Symphony Orchestra, David Epstein conducting, released by Vox Turnabout

Classic Film Scores LP albums *The Sea Hawk, Elizabeth and Essex*, and *Captain Blood* re-released by RCA

November: Symphony in F sharp major performed by the St. Louis Symphony Orchestra, Christopher Keene conducting

December 5: Korngold Commemorative Concert at Library of Congress.

1982 Cold-cast bronze portrait-bust of Korngold by Alexander J. Stoddart (Paisley, Scotland) completed, and displayed at Philharmonic Hall, Liverpool, on 2 March

2 March: U.K. première of the Symphony in F sharp major by the Royal Liverpool Philharmonic Orchestra, Marek Janowski conducting, in Liverpool, organised and with a pre-concert talk on Korngold by Brendan G. Carroll

September: Korngold's Sinfonietta tape-recorded by the BBC Philharmonic, Edward Downes conducting

September: Violin Concerto, Itzhak Perlman, soloist, Pittsburgh

Symphony Orchestra, André Previn conducting, released by EMI (Digital)

11 October: The Erich Wolfgang Korngold Society founded in Paisley, Scotland

1983   5 February: Première of a season of *Die tote Stadt* by the Deutsche Oper Belin, directed and produced by Professor Götz Friedrich, with Karan Armstong and James King

March: Sinfonietta broadcast on BBC Radio 3

March: *Der Ring des Polykrates* performed at the Manhattan School of Music, New York

May: Korngold programme, 'From Vienna to Hollywood', presented in the 1983 Paisley Festival

August: Violin Concerto performed by the Chicago Symphony Orchestra

September: RIAS Berlin radio retrospective of Korngold's works, including the Concerto for Piano (Left-Hand) and Orchestra, Steven de Groote, soloist, and the Sinfonietta, in an orchestral concert conducted by Gerd Albrecht, as well as two chamber concerts, including the Piano Trio and the String Sextet. Varese Sarabande record the Piano Trio, the String Sextet, and the Sinfonietta for release in 1984

December: *The Adventures of Robin Hood* released by Varese Sarabande

1984   January: the Deutsche Oper Berlin announce further performances of *Die tote Stadt*

January: *Magic Fire* released by Varese Sarabande

8 February: Violin Concerto, Ingo Klöckl, soloist, performed with Hessian State Orchestra, Wiesbaden, Siegfried Kohler conducting

July/August: *Violanta* in new production by Santa Fe Opera, New Mexico, U.S.A.

August: two concerts of Korngold's film music scheduled by the Detroit Symphony Orchestra

November: Violin Concerto, Christian Altenburger, soloist, scheduled with the Chicago Symphony Orchestra, Leonard Slatkin conducting

1985   15 April: Violin Concerto, Ulf Hoelscher, soloist, in Cologne, West Germany

May: *Sursum Corda* scheduled for performance by the Scottish Sinfonia, Neil Mantle conducting, in Edinburgh

September: Concerto for Piano (Left-Hand) and Orchestra, Gary Graffman, soloist, scheduled with the New York Philharmonic Orchestra, Zubin Mehta conducting (U.S. premiere)

SELECTED DISCOGRAPHY

N.B. A comprehensive discography, prepared by Mr. Roger Wilmut, will be published in the full-length biography of Korngold. Meanwhile, the records listed below are the most recent and available.

I. Chamber Works

1. Piano Sonata No.2 in E major, Op.2/*Märchenbilder*, Op.3. Antonin Kubalek, piano. Genesis GS 1055 (U.S.A.).

2. Violin Sonata in G major, Op.6. Endre Granat, violin; Harold Gray, piano. Orion ORS 74166 (U.S.A., 1974).

3. String Quartet No.2 in E-flat major, Op.26. New World Quartet. Vox (box set) SVBX 5109 (1978).

4. Piano Sonata No.3 in C major, Op.25. Harold Gray, piano. Genesis GS 1063 (U.S.A.).

II. Lieder

1. *Abschiedslieder*, Op.14. Rosette Anday, accompanied by Korngold, piano (1924). Reissued on Preisser LV32 (Austria).

III. Orchestral Works

1. *Schauspiel Overture* in B major, Op.4. M.I.T. Symphony Orchestra, David Epstein conducting. Turnabout TV 34760 (1978).

2. *Much Ado about Nothing* Suite, Violin Concerto, and Theme and Variations. South German Radio Orchestra of Stuttgart, Willy Mattes conducting. Ulf Hoelscher, soloist. EMI EMD 5515 (in U.S.A., Angel S-36999).

3. Violin Concerto in D major, Op.35. Los Angeles Philharmonic, Alfred Wallenstein conducting; Jascha Heifetz, soloist. RCA LSB 4105 (U.K.); LM 1782 (U.S.A.); 26.41236 (West Gemany).

4. Violin Concerto in D major, Op.35. Pittsburgh Symphony Orchestra, André Previn conducting; Itzhak Perlman, soloist. HMV ASD 4206 (in U.S.A., Angel DS 37770).

5. Cello Concerto in C major, Op.35. National Philharmonic Orchestra, Charles Gerhardt conducting; Francisco Gabarro, soloist. RCA ARLI-0185.

6. Symphony in F sharp major, Op.40. Munich Philharmonic Orchestra, Rudolf Kempe conducting. RCA ARLI-0443.

7. *Tomorrow*, Op.33. Tone Poem for Contralto, Chorus and Orchestra. Norma Procter, contralto, and the Ambrosian Singers; National Philharmonic Orchestra, Charles Gerhardt conducting. RCA SER 5664.

IV. Operas

1. *Violanta*, Op.8. Eva Marton, Siegfried Jerusalem, Walter Berry; Munich Radio Orchestra and Chorus, Marek Janowski conducting. CBS 79229.

2. *Die tote Stadt*, Op.12. Carol Neblett, René Kollo, Hermann Prey, Benjamin Luxon; Bavarian Radio Chorus, Tölzer Boys Choir; Munich Radio Orchestra, Erich Leinsdorf conducting. RCA RL 01199 FK (West Germany: only German sets are now available).

V. Film Music

1. *The Sea Hawk*. National Philharmonic Orchestra, Charles Gerhardt conducting. RCA: LSC 3330 (U.S.A.); RCA: SER 5664 (U.K.).

2. *Captain Blood*. National Philharmonic Orchestra, Charles Gerhardt conducting. RCA ARLI-0912.

3. *Elizabeth and Essex*. National Philharmonic Orchestra, Charles Gerhardt conducting. RCA ARLI-0185.

4. *Kings Row Suite*. National Philharmonic Orchestra, Charles Gerhardt conducting. Chalfont Digital SDG 305.

5. *The Adventures of Robin Hood*. The Utah Symphony Orchestra, Varujan Kojian conducting. Varese Sarabande 704.180.

VI. Miscellaneous

1. *Korngold conducts and plays Korngold.* Includes: *Much Ado about Nothing* Suite, Piano Improvisations on *Violanta, Die tote Stadt* and *Die Kathrin.* Austrian State Symphony Orchestra. Recorded in 1951.
Varese Sarabande VC 81040.

SELECTED BIBLIOGRAPHY

1. Adler, Gusti. *Max Reinhardt – sein Leben*. Salzburg, 1964.

2. Berl, Heinrich. *Das Judentum in der Musik*. Berlin, 1926.

3. Brockhoven, J. van. 'A precocious musical genius,' *The Musical Observer*. (New York), Vol. 9, 1919, pp.102-109.

4. Chevalley, Heinrich. *Hundert Jahre Hamburger Stadttheater*. Hamburg, 1927.

5. _____. *'Das Wunder der Heliane,' Musikwelt* (Hamburg), November 1927.

6. Flindell, E. Fred. 'Paul Wittgenstein: Einige Dokumente der Sammlung P. Wittgenstein,' *Die Musikforschung*. Kassel, 1962.

7. _____. 'Paul Wittgenstein: Patron and Pianist,' *The Music Review* (London), Vol. 32, No.2, May 1972.

8. Hoffmann, Rudolf Stefan. *Erich Wolfgang Korngold*. Vienna, 1922.

9. Hollander, Felix. *Lebendiges Theater*. Fischer-Verlag, 1932.

10. Humperdinck, Engelbert. *Sang und Klang im 19th und 20th Jahrhundert*. Berlin 1912.

11. Kapp, Julius. *Die Oper der Gegenwart*. Berlin, 1922.

12. Korngold, Julius. *Child Prodigy*. New York: Willard, 1945.

13. Korngold, Luzi. *Erich Wolfgang Korngold*. Vienna, 1967. Vienna: Lafite-Verlag, 1967.

14. Mahler-Werfel, Alma. *Mein Leben*. Fischer-Verlag, 1960.

15. Prawy, Marcel. *The Vienna Opera*. Vienna, 1965.

16. Reinhardt, Gottfried. *The Genius: A Memoir of Max Reinhardt*. New York: Alfred A. Knopf, 1979.

17. Schmidt, Leopold. *Musikleben der Gegenwart*. Berlin, 1922.

18. Seidl, Arthur. *Neuzeitliche Tondichter und Zeitgenossische Tonkunstler*. Regensburg, 1926.

19. _____.*Studien zur Wertungsforschung – Alexander Zemlinsky*. Universal Edition, 1976.

20. Specht, Richard. *Thematic Analysis of the Sinfonietta*. Mainz: Schott, 1914.

21. _____. *Thematische Führer zu Erich W. Korngolds Opern-einaktern 'Violanta' und 'Der Ring des Polykrates'*. Mainz: Schott, 1916.

22. Thomas, Tony. *Music from the Movies*. A.S. Barnes/Tantivy, 1973, pp. 123-140.

23. Weingartner, Felix. *Lebenserinnerungen*. Zürich, 1929.

24. Wenzel, Joachim. *Gesichte der Hamburger Oper 1678-1978*. Hamburg, 1979.

Further Reading:

1. *Collected Critiques of the First Performances of the Sinfonietta*. Mainz: Schott, 1915.

2. *Collected Critiques of the Performances of the One-Act Operas for the 50th Anniversary of the Vienna Opera in May 1919*. Mainz: Schott, 1920.

3. Endler, Franz. *Julius Korngold und die 'Neue Freie Presse'*. Unpublished doctoral dissertation. University of Vienna, October 1981.

4. Korngold, Julius. *Postludes in Major and Minor*. Unpublished memoirs. In the archive of the *Neue Freie Presse*, Vienna.

5. For critiques of performances of Korngold's works, 1910-1933, consult:

    a. *Signale für die Musikalische Welt*, published weekly in Berlin.

    b. *Die Musik*, Stuttgart.

    c. *Der Merker*, Vienna

d. *Musikleben*, Hamburg

e. *Die Neue Freie Presse*, Vienna.

BRENDAN G. CARROLL, born in Southport, England, is preparing a major biography of Korngold. He left music teaching in 1981 to join a Southern Leisure Company, and since 1983, has become a full-time free-lance broadcaster in the North West. Besides contributing the career article on Korngold to the 1981 edition of *Grove's Dictionary of Music and Musicians*, he has had numerous other articles on Korngold published in a variety of international periodicals. He is the President of The Erich Wolfgang Korngold Society.

The Erich Wolfgang Korngold Society

4 Townhead Terrace,
Paisley, Renfrewshire PA1 2AX,
Scotland, U.K.